Eye of the Storm

The Devastation, Resiliency and Restoration of Tuscaloosa, Alabama

Presented by

The Tuscaloosa News

Copyright© 2011 by The Tuscaloosa News • All Rights Reserved • ISBN: 978-1-59725-330-7
All rights reserved. No part of this book may be reproduced, stored in a retrieval system or transmitted in any form or by any means, electronic, mechanical, photocopying, recording or otherwise, without prior written permission of the copyright owner or the publisher.
Published by Pediment Publishing, a division of The Pediment Group, Inc. www.pediment.com Printed in Canada.

FOREWORD

If April 27, 2011 was not the most calamitous day in the history of Tuscaloosa, you would have to look back at least 146 years to find its equal. The monster tornado changed the city surely as much as the Union Army cavalry did in April 1865, when 1,500 troops under the command of Brig. Gen. John Croxton burned nearly every building on the University of Alabama campus.

Then, as now, the people of Tuscaloosa mourned, dug in and rebuilt.

Images of the storm, captured on television cameras and cell phones, and seen around the world, rallied support not only for Tuscaloosa but also for other areas of the state raked by 62 tornadoes, part of a larger outbreak climatologists are studying as the "Southern States Outbreak" that killed at least 325 people in six states. President Barak Obama quickly came, as did professional athletes and other celebrities, to lend encouragement. Church groups and other charitable assistance poured in. Kenny Chesney and the band Alabama held benefit concerts at the city's new amphitheater.

Tuscaloosa, where it has sometimes felt like the center of the universe on the day of a big football game at Bryant-Denny Stadium, found itself the focus of attention on a much larger stage. The stakes are much bigger, the challenges are difficult to grasp even yet, but the opportunities may be even greater.

What will Tuscaloosa become?

Maybe part of the answer to that question lies back in the rubble of April 27. This book is an effort to take you back there with us, to recall the scenes of devastation and many acts of bravery and humanity that followed. Our photographers and reporters have been there at every step, watching the tornado approach and following in its wake, standing beside those who had lost everything and chronicling those who came to assist. Never have we felt our particular duty more clearly and urgently.

A new vision for Tuscaloosa is rising. It will contain a portion of its past even as it reaches to the future; for an example, look at what the University of Alabama has become over the past century and half. If there is a single theme to emerge it is this: connection. The storm blew away boundaries that kept us apart and brought us together in wonderful new ways. We mourn those whom we have lost, but we are committed to honoring them as we move forward. ∎

TABLE OF CONTENTS

THE DISASTER 7

RESPONSE 33

ALBERTA FAMILY 69

ROBERT REED 75

RECOVERY 81

THOSE WHO DIED 117

AMPHITHEATER BENEFITS 119

BEFORE AND AFTER 124

ACKNOWLEDGMENTS 128

THE DISASTER

APRIL 27, 2011 | JASON MORTON, STAFF WRITER

The threat had been lingering for days.

A half-dozen miles above the earth, the polar jetstream of frigid air racing at more than 100 miles an hour dipped into West Alabama. It arrived on an unseasonably hot, summer-like day as Tuscaloosa children played on the ground below.

Schools had cancelled classes that day and many businesses closed early because weather forecasters had been warning that severe weather was almost certain.

Less than two weeks earlier, on April 15, a band of strong winds and small tornadoes brought a wave of damage across east Tuscaloosa. No one was killed, but residents had been reminded of nature's power.

The threat on April 27 was expected to materialize in the afternoon, but a predawn storm already had hit Tuscaloosa County like a sucker punch. Maybe the worst had already passed.

But at 5:09 p.m., a supercell storm that already had spun deadly twisters across Mississippi crossed the western edge of Tuscaloosa County. People who had been following weather reports on television and the Internet all day began reaching out to friends and family. It was time to find your safe place.

As a half-mile wide tornado descended, there was no safe place in its path. Lights flickered and went out. Television screens went dark. Sirens filled the air.

The city's brick- and concrete-fortified disaster response center on 35th Street in west Tuscaloosa was one of the first buildings torn apart. From there, on a ragged diagonal through the center of the city, through public housing and historic neighborhoods, across commercial centers and mobile home parks, the tornado brought destruction.

People huddled in bathtubs and closets saw their homes blow apart around them. People clung together but were pulled apart. Cars went flying. Boats sailed through air.

At Hobby Lobby in Wood Square, 10 employees and about as many customers held tightly to each other in a back corner of the building as the tornado passed overhead. Employee Alison Tucker thought to herself, "My God, let us survive."

After another worker spotted the tornado heading toward the shopping center off McFarland Boulevard, everyone in the store ran to a breakroom in the back. Tucker could feel the air pressure shift, and tile began to peel away from the roof.

A manager held the door of the breakroom closed as the tornado tried to pull it open. The tornado finally won, ripping the door open. The manager dove back and grabbed a woman who seemed to be slipping away.

"Somehow, the walls stayed up," Tucker said hours later. "For some reason they stayed. "I don't know

---

OPPOSITE: The tornado, later determined to be a category EF4 with winds approaching 200 mph, moves through Tuscaloosa on Wednesday, April 27, 2011.

Dusty Compton/The Tuscaloosa News

ABOVE: Rosedale Court residents comfort one another and look to salvage belongings after the tornado destroyed their homes.

Kelly Lambert/The Tuscaloosa News

why, but they did."

As the roar of the storm died away, it was replaced by the cries of the injured. Survivors emerged into unfamiliar landscapes and began pulling trapped neighbors free of the rubble.

Those with cuts and other wounds who still could walk began making their way toward DCH Regional Medical Center, which had been grazed but not directly hit. Many of those who couldn't walk were carried by strangers on doors used as makeshift stretchers.

In Alberta, firefighters, police officers and residents stood on a pile of rubble that had been an apartment building. They used chainsaws, floor jacks and their bare hands to lift walls and debris that had fallen on top of a University of Alabama student who was trapped several feet underneath.

The woman yelled she couldn't feel her legs, but they kept digging. As night fell, the rescue effort continued.

First responders didn't attend to the dead. Instead, they busied themselves with caring for the living as survivors placed blankets over the bodies of neighbors lying in the ruins of destroyed homes.

"The earth went moving," said Fred Jackson, 48, who had cowered in the bathroom of his home at 915 Alberta Drive.

"Roots were being pulled up. Everything was moving. The house is destroyed. We had to get out through a window," Jackson said, joining scores of people bleeding, limping or being carried away from the devastation.

Those on cell phones who were lucky enough to get through to a 911 operator were told to take care of themselves. No ambulance, they were told, would be coming.

Less than five hours later, a stoic Mayor Walt Maddox announced that 32 people had been confirmed dead. In the days and weeks that followed, the death toll in Tuscaloosa grew to 42 people who suffered injuries in the storm. Additional names were added as others died from related causes, bringing list to 51 names as of Sept. 20. Across Alabama, at least 250 people died from the 62 confirmed tornados that struck the state that day.

The city's damage assessments began pouring in almost as soon as the winds died down, and the list sounded more like a disaster movie script than real-life Tuscaloosa.

Thousands of homes and buildings — it eventually would total more than 5,000 — had been turned into rubble.

A police precinct and two elementary schools — the city's Alberta Elementary School and Holt Elementary School in the county system — were destroyed along with the city garbage and debris removal trucks.

The Red Cross and Salvation Army headquarters had taken hits, a fire station was smashed and a sewage treatment plant was badly damaged.

As water delivery to east Tuscaloosa began to fail, it became clear that should a fire break out in that part of the city, it could not be stopped.

"That's your first 20 minutes," Maddox would say weeks after the storm had passed. "I'll never forget it." ■

LEFT: Laura Yerby helps search through the wreckage of a neighbor's home on Recreation Area Road near Eagle Cove Marina, about one mile east of Tuscaloosa. Two people lost their lives in the neighborhood. *Robert Sutton/The Tuscaloosa News*

BELOW: A scene of destruction at Rosedale Court, a public housing development in Tuscaloosa.

Kelly Lambert/The Tuscaloosa News

ABOVE: A woman sits on the remains of her home in Rosedale Court. *Kelly Lambert/The Tuscaloosa News*

OPPOSITE: A man runs through the devastation of Rosedale Court for safety as word spreads that another storm is on its way after a tornado tore through Alabama. A second tornado did not materialize in Tuscaloosa that evening. *Kelly Lambert/The Tuscaloosa News*

ABOVE: Stephanie Hines, left, takes in the destruction at her mother's house in the Rosedale Court community. *Kelly Lambert/The Tuscaloosa News*

RIGHT: People aid a friend near the Rosedale Court. *Kelly Lambert/The Tuscaloosa News*

FAR RIGHT: Rosemarie Roberts is aided by Charles Redick, left, and Nathan Reese after her home was destroyed by the tornado. *Kelly Lambert/The Tuscaloosa News*

LEFT: Oma Phurrough is transported through the damage on 15th Street. *Michelle Lepianka Carter/The Tuscaloosa News*

FAR LEFT: People walk through rubble left of homes and businesses in Cedar Crest a few minutes after the tornado hit. *Michelle Lepianka Carter/The Tuscaloosa News*

BELOW: A member of the Tuscaloosa Police Department directs traffic at the intersection of 15th Street and McFarland Boulevard. *Michelle Lepianka Carter/The Tuscaloosa News*

The Tuscaloosa News

Tuscaloosa, Northport, West Alabama — Thursday, April 28, 2011 — 50¢

WWW.TUSCALOOSANEWS.COM

TORNADO RAVAGES CITY

FATAL STORM
At least 15 people killed in Tuscaloosa area

NEIGHBORHOODS
Rosedale Court, Alberta suffer massive damage

STATE OF EMERGENCY
President approves aid; governor sends Guard

SCHOOLS
Tuscaloosa city and county schools closed

STAFF PHOTO | DUSTY COMPTON

For photos, video and updates, visit www.tuscaloosanews.com. Tuscaloosa residents standing on Dr. Edward Hillard Drive near the intersection of 15th Street look into the Cedar Crest neighborhood where cars are upended and buildings are destroyed in Tuscaloosa on Wednesday. A strong tornado moved through the city in the afternoon.

West Ala. suffers death, destruction

By Jason Morton
Staff Writer

TUSCALOOSA | At least 15 people are dead and more than 100 injured in the wake of a devastating tornado that hit the city late Wednesday afternoon, destroying thousands of homes, businesses and other structures.

That was the sobering message a stoic Mayor Walt Maddox delivered Wednesday night amid the aftermath of a series of storms that killed 72 people in four states.

"This afternoon, Tuscaloosa was devastated by a tornado which has created death and destruction across our city," Maddox began. "To my fellow citizens who are hurting tonight, in the days, weeks and months ahead, our city will rise to meet these challenges by dedicating every available resource."

Among those resources was a host of emergency powers temporarily granted Maddox by a unanimous vote of the City Council. All but one member — Councilman Kip Tyner, whose District 5 was among the hardest hit — was in at...

STAFF PHOTO | MICHELLE LEPIANKA CARTER

STAFF PHOTO | DUSTY COMPTON
TOP: A large tornado is seen moving down 15th Street in Tuscaloosa at 5:13 p.m. on Wednesday.

Survivors crawl from the rubble

Staff report

Muffled screams could be heard from a pile of debris that used to be an apartment complex at Arlington Square in Alberta on Wednesday.

Firefighters, police officers and Alberta residents stood atop the pile, digging with their hands, using chain saws to cut through planks and using floor jacks to lift the walls that had fallen on top of a University of Alabama student who was trapped several feet under the debris.

The woman yelled that she couldn't feel her legs.

They kept digging, but as night fell, her rescuers still had not been able to free her from the rubble.

The tornado that hit Tuscaloosa on Wednesday devastated the Alberta community.

Few, if any, houses and buildings remained standing.

Trees and power lines were strewn everywhere.

Cars were flipped over, stairwells were twisted and people were trapped in their homes, calling to first responders for help.

People sifted through the remains of their homes looking for anything they could salvage.

The air was filled with the

SEE SURVIVORS | 7A

EDITOR'S NOTE
The Tuscaloosa News lost power in the storm, so today's edition was...

INSIDE: VOL. 193 NO. 118 | 4 Sections

ABOVE: Businesses and homes along 15th Street were destroyed as the tornado moved through the city. *Dusty Compton/The Tuscaloosa News*

OPPOSITE RIGHT: Signs and trees were twisted beyond recognition by the powerful storm.

Michelle Lepianka Carter/The Tuscaloosa News

RIGHT: Chris Jordan consoles his fiance, Stephanie Prickett, after the storm. The couple was at Jordan's apartment at University Downs when the tornado hit.
Michelle Lepianka Carter/The Tuscaloosa News

OPPOSITE: Citizens walk down McFarland Boulevard surveying the damage immediately after the storm. *Michelle Lepianka Carter/The Tuscaloosa News*

ABOVE: A displaced family is assisted by emergency responders near 15th Street. *Dusty Compton/The Tuscaloosa News*

RIGHT: A woman and man hold onto each other at the corner of 15th Street and McFarland Boulevard after the storm. *Michelle Lepianka Carter/The Tuscaloosa News*

FAR RIGHT: Pearline G. Hinton, left, and her son Kendrell Dwayne Hinton, 16, flee the remains of their home in Rosedale Court after hearing word that another storm was on its way after a tornado tore through Tuscaloosa. A second tornado did not arrive that evening, however. *Kelly Lambert/The Tuscaloosa News*

ABOVE: Firefighters search a business for survivors after the tornado leveled the Cash Depot on 15th Street.

Jason Harless/The Tuscaloosa News

LEFT: A man walks on top of houses reduced to rubble along 10th Street.

Michelle Lepianka Carter/The Tuscaloosa News

OPPOSITE: Tiffany Price collects some of her clothes from her house in Rosedale Court.

Kelly Lambert/The Tuscaloosa News

ABOVE: A woman holds a baby amid the wreckage of destroyed homes as others try to salvage anything they can from the destroyed residences.
Michelle Lepianka Carter/The Tuscaloosa News

RIGHT: Netricia Stokes, left, and Jasmine Brown, holding 3-month-old Kyleigh Stokes, walk down 10th Street near Rosedale Court with Torace Stokes and Keldrick Crews the day after the storm. The group was helping friends carry belongings out of their destroyed home. *Michelle Lepianka Carter/The Tuscaloosa News*

FAR RIGHT: Rescue and recovery teams sift through the wreckage in Alberta and Holt following the deadly tornadoes. *Jamie Cicatiello/The Tuscaloosa News*

ABOVE: Of the 188 housing units at Rosedale Court, 100 were destroyed, leaving 96 families homeless. The entire complex was later razed. *Dusty Compton/The Tuscaloosa News*

LEFT: The Charleston Square apartment complex, near 10th Avenue, sustained heavy damage.

Dusty Compton/The Tuscaloosa News

OPPOSITE: The path the tornado took can be clearly seen as a gray swath extending across Tuscaloosa east to the horizon.

Dusty Compton/The Tuscaloosa News

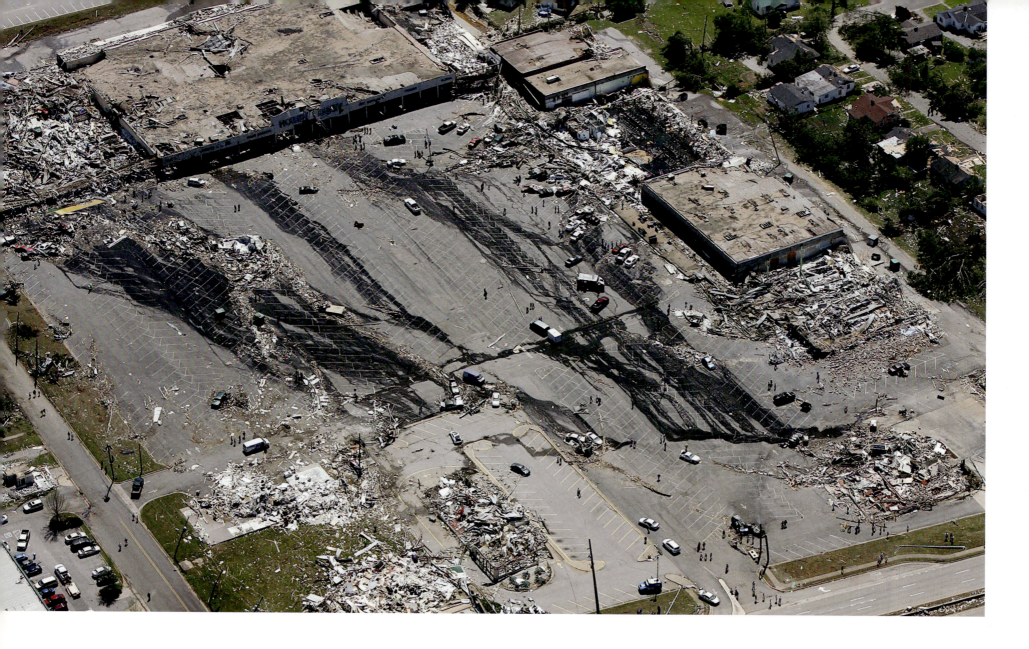

ABOVE: The Wood Square shopping center, where Hobby Lobby and Big Lots stores were located, was flattened beyond recognition. *Dusty Compton/The Tuscaloosa News*

OPPOSITE: The intersection of McFarland Boulevard and 15th Street in Tuscaloosa was among the busiest retail corners in the city.

Dusty Compton/The Tuscaloosa News

ABOVE: While six residents of Rosedale Court died in the storm, city officials were relieved that the death toll was not higher. *Dusty Compton/The Tuscaloosa News*

RIGHT: Several people rode out the storm in their boats at Eagle Cove Marina in Peterson. Several boats and the marina itself suffered extensive damage.

Robert Sutton/The Tuscaloosa News

OPPOSITE: People sit in the doorway of a destroyed home in the Cedar Crest neighborhood surrounded by debris the day after the storm.

Michelle Lepianka Carter/The Tuscaloosa News

RESPONSE

MAY 4, 2011 | STEPHANIE TAYLOR, STAFF WRITER

One of the first signs that Tuscaloosa was beginning to move from crisis to response came on May 4, when classes resumed for students in the city and county public school systems.

A teacher asked her elementary students to describe how the week before had affected them.

"We cooked for people," one student wrote. "We helped my cousin get a car. We have people sharing my house, my toys and my bedroom. We shared food with strangers. We donated clothes and shoes."

The next line written referred to the difficulty people experienced as they navigated a debris-filled city where entire neighborhoods were blocked off and guarded by men in military uniforms and police officers with guns at their hips.

But the student's observation was true in a greater sense than intended: "We have to find new ways to get places."

Finding new ways to get places. New ways to get things done without going through the established channels. It's that spirit — one of regular people seeing a need and doing something about it — that came to define the community's response to the tornado that destroyed so much.

Minutes after the tornado hit, people left the wreckage of their homes to search for survivors.

An untold number of survivors canvassed the streets, searching for people who were trapped. There were people like Robert Reed, the manager of Crescent Mobile Home Estates, who pulled 12 people from piles of concrete, lumber and other heavy debris. There was Brandon Reid, a 21-year-old University of Alabama student who went from home to home in the Forest Lake neighborhood looking for survivors.

"I really don't know what I'm doing," he told a reporter, in a shaky voice just minutes after the storm.

"I just know that Jesus said to love your neighbor as yourself, and I know I would want help if I were trapped in my house."

Pickup trucks became makeshift ambulances, with drivers rushing people they had never met to DCH Regional Medical Center, which sits just feet from the storm's path.

"People didn't just stand on their porch and say 'poor me.' They got out there and they helped their neighbors," said Tuscaloosa Fire and Rescue Assistant Chief George White. "I think that's why the death toll wasn't higher than it was."

Police, firefighters and paramedics spread out across the affected areas, leaving the dead where they lay and searching for people who could be saved. Road and bridge crews traveled the streets to clear mountains of debris to make way for rescuers. In the county, deputies walked for more than a mile through

OPPOSITE: Rows of cots line the floor of the gymnasium at the Red Cross shelter inside the Belk Activity Center in Tuscaloosa, Tuesday, May 10. *Dusty Compton/The Tuscaloosa News*

downed oak trees and power lines to reach a home on a bluff near Hurricane Creek to aid a woman with two broken arms and a life-threatening head injury. The department's helicopter performed a dangerous landing to rescue the woman and transport her to DCH, likely saving her life.

Hundreds of people were treated at the hospital that night. Staff didn't even take people's names; they treated them and sent them on their way. One nurse described the experience as "organized chaos."

Officials didn't take long to mobilize. President Barack Obama declared a state of emergency that night. National Guard units arrived before sunrise the next day. Obama and First Lady Michelle toured Alberta and Holt that Friday, two days after the tornado struck.

"I've never seen destruction like this," Obama said.

On the night of the tornado, the Clear Channel radio stations that broadcast from Tuscaloosa became a lifeline for people seeking and sharing information. The stations took live calls and became the only source of information for many people who were left with no phone service or power after the tornado.

The first few hours, callers talked about where roads were blocked or asked if anyone had information about their loved ones. In the days that followed, people and organizations began to call with needs for food, water and supplies that were often fulfilled within minutes of broadcast.

Response was hampered because the tornado struck the buildings of three key disaster response agencies: the Tuscaloosa County Emergency Management Agency, the Salvation Army and the Red Cross of West Alabama. The EMA dispatched calls out of the Tuscaloosa Police Department immediately following the storm, and all three found temporary headquarters from which to base operations.

Groups of people mobilized with the help of Facebook and Twitter. Organizations like We Are T-Town and Toomers For Tuscaloosa collected donations and drove door-to-door in the stricken areas to hand out clothing, food, water and medical supplies. Soma Church in Holt became a hub for volunteers and victims in the Crescent Lane area of Holt. Holy Spirit Catholic Church became an unintended shelter where Hispanic victims received aid and were eventually able to meet with the consulates of Mexico and Guatemala.

Actor Charlie Sheen visited on May 2, five days after the tornado, and pledged to raise money for Tuscaloosa after touring Alberta. Singers Hank Williams Jr., Ruben Studdard and Lance Bass volunteered. NY Giants player Justin Tuck, NBA players Josh Powell of the Atlanta Hawks and Dwight

ABOVE: Tuscaloosa Mayor Walt Maddox, right, speaks with President Barack Obama as they tour damaged areas in the Alberta area of Tuscaloosa, Friday, April 29. Obama, along with Alabama Governor Robert Bentley, Maddox, U.S. Senators Jeff Sessions and Richard Shelby, and other local and national dignitaries visited Tuscaloosa.

Dusty Compton / The Tuscaloosa News

Howard of the Orlando Magic, former University of Alabama players Joe Namath, Julio Jones, Mark Ingram, Javier Arenas, Greg McElroy, Jay Barker and his wife, country singer Sara Evans, visited. Many of the celebrities volunteered in shelters, spoke with victims or helped sort donations.

Tuscaloosa was featured on television news programs, radio broadcasts and newspapers around the world. Volunteers and donations came in from all over the country. Many businesses in Tuscaloosa gave their employees days off to spend volunteering.

As of early July, 18,639 people had registered with the city's Volunteer Reception Center and had logged 129,247 hours. It's likely that many more people have volunteered many more hours, and will continue to in the months and years it takes Tuscaloosa to recover from the disaster. ■

FAR LEFT: Tuscaloosa Mayor Walt Maddox visits 15th Street the day after the tornado.

Michelle Lepianka Carter/The Tuscaloosa News

ABOVE: President Barack Obama speaks with Alabama Gov. Robert Bentley, right, and U.S. Sen. Richard Shelby in Tuscaloosa on Friday, April 29.
Dusty Compton / The Tuscaloosa News

TOP RIGHT: Bentley talks with former University of Alabama head football coach Gene Stallings while viewing damage before a press conference near the corner of 15th Street and McFarland Boulevard on Thursday, April 28. *Michelle Lepianka Carter / The Tuscaloosa News*

RIGHT: Tuscaloosa City Councilman Kip Tyner talks with University of Alabama student Angela Palmer and her family in Alberta about damage. Palmer's family came from Atlanta to pick her up.
Michelle Lepianka Carter / The Tuscaloosa News

ABOVE: First Lady Michelle Obama speaks with Alabama First Lady Dianne Bentley as President Barack Obama speaks with Alabama Gov. Robert Bentley in Tuscaloosa, Friday, April 29. *Dusty Compton/The Tuscaloosa News*

LEFT: President Barack Obama consoles Holt Elementary Principal Debbie Crawford as Sen. Richard Shelby, left, and Gov. Robert Bentley, right, look on at the school Friday, April 29. Holt Elementary was being used as a temporary shelter. *Dusty Compton/The Tuscaloosa News*

OPPOSITE: President Obama meets with Alberta residents. *Dusty Compton/The Tuscaloosa News*

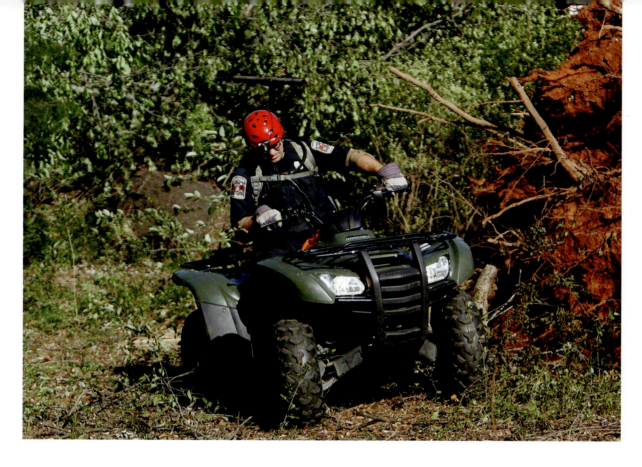

ABOVE: An Alabama state trooper performs search and rescue in the Holt community Friday, April 29.

Michelle Lepianka Carter/The Tuscaloosa News

RIGHT: Residents carry supplies through a distribution area set up by volunteers at the former Locklear Dodge dealership on Saturday, April 30.

Michelle Lepianka Carter/The Tuscaloosa News

ABOVE: Bev and Craig Dubois sign up to volunteer inside St. Matthias' Espiscopal Church. *Michelle Lepianka Carter/The Tuscaloosa News*

ABOVE: Lenny and Donna Holbrook and other members of the congregation pray during a church service at Alberta Baptist Church that was held in the parking lot next to the church on Sunday morning, four days after the storm. The church suffered major structural damage from the storm. *T.G. Paschal/The Tuscaloosa News*

8 PAGES OF PHOTOS	HELP	SCHOOLS	CLEANUP	IN TODAY'S PAPER
Images showing the aftermath of Wednesday's deadly tornado in Tuscaloosa. **Section I**	Where to go if you want to volunteer, or need help recovering from the storm | **2A**	Alberta and University Place students to transfer to different schools; schools collect donations | **3A**	City to begin removing debris Wednesday | **5A** **CLOSINGS** List of whats open, closed | **2A**	COUPONS WORTH **$467** In most areas

The Tuscaloosa News

Tuscaloosa, Northport, West Alabama — Sunday, May 1, 2011 — $1.50
WWW.TUSCALOOSANEWS.COM

Help comes from near, far

Volunteers hand out supplies at the former Locklear dealership to people affected by the April 27 tornado. STAFF PHOTOS | MICHELLE LEPIANKA CARTER

By Wayne Grayson and Andrew Carroll
Staff writers

TUSCALOOSA

"Krispy Kreme!" the man shouted. "Where did y'all get Krispy Kreme?"

He ran over to the large white Ford pickup with excitement and took the box containing a dozen doughnuts before quickly opening it to see and smell the pastries shining in the afternoon sun.

"That felt like Christmas," Sam Shuttlesworth said Saturday, watching the man walk back to his damaged home on Crescent Lane in Holt. He climbed into the passenger-side seat of the truck and closed the door before the smile faded from his face as he looked out of his window.

The view overlooked a steep drop. Below were thousands of downed trees all pointed toward Holt, the lasting mark of the deadly tornado that ripped through Tuscaloosa on April 27.

Shuttlesworth, 24, a University of Alabama alumnus living in Birmingham, and his two friends, Robert Beasley, 25, and Daniel Wood, 24, also UA alums, spent most of Saturday delivering hot meals, drinks — and even a few Krispy Kreme doughnuts via Birmingham — to victims and volunteers in Alberta and Holt. Their effort was part of UA Greek Relief Fund, a joint effort between Greek social fraternities and sororities to aid in the recovery effort.

Students met at the Delta Kappa Epsilon and Beta Theta Pi fraternity houses where food, drinks, clothing, baby and school supplies were dropped off and hot meals were prepared. Students packed vehicles full of the supplies and delivered them across the city.

Former UA Student Government Association president and DKE member James Fowler said Saturday that the effort began when DKE members learned that the university had can-

> "My heart goes out to everybody who has children here and those that haven't been recovered yet. That's just devastating. I don't know how they can possibly deal with that."
> Debbie Leverett, mother of a UA student who survived the storm

Have you been to the hardest hit areas of Tuscaloosa? Visit www.tuscaloosanews.com to vote in our poll.

celed final exams and commencement ceremonies.

"With the school year essentially over, we all realized we had a kitchen full of food that we had stocked for end-of-the-school-year events that was going to go to waste," Fowler said. "So instead of letting that happen, we really wanted to get that food and drink out to the people who need it."

Fowler said the fraternity then asked their fellow fraternities and sororities to help out beginning Friday. By Friday night, Fowler said they realized they needed to double their efforts, and that's exactly what they

See **HELP** | 10A

MAYOR: DEATH TOLL MAY RISE; CURFEW REMAINS

By Brian Reynolds
Staff Writer

TUSCALOOSA | The Tuscaloosa Police Department will begin today releasing the names of those killed in the April 27 tornado, while the sheriff's department is expected to release names of the dead in the county, Mayor Walt Maddox said Saturday night.

The official death toll remains at 39, but the number of injured and missing remains fluid as search, rescue and recovery work continues in Tuscaloosa.

The number of injuries reported by DCH Regional Medical Center has risen to more than 1,000. However, many injuries, especially those immediately after the storm, may not be included in that number.

April 27 marked the second-deadliest day of twisters in U.S. history, leaving 342 people dead across seven states — including 250 in Alabama.

As of 9 a.m. Saturday, 570 people in Tuscaloosa had been reported missing, but that number had fallen to 434 by the evening. Officials were able to remove 234 names from the list of missing, but more missing person reports keep the number high.

"I do continue to grow concerned about this number," Maddox said Saturday night. "I was very hopeful that I could come out here tonight

Mayor Walt Maddox talks to people in the Save-A-Lot parking lot in Alberta on Saturday.

See **MAYOR** | 12A

Alberta official Kip Tyner hit hard by city's damage

By Stephanie Taylor
Staff Writer

TUSCALOOSA | Kip Tyner is almost as devastated as the landscape of the Alberta community in the aftermath of the April 27 tornado.

He has spent the past 15 years on the City Council working to improve the area. He has transformed the hook-er-pole lined and pothole-filled road to one with decorative lamp posts, trees and underground utilities. He has fought to bring businesses to the area and keep the post office open

City Councilman Kip Tyner has been working to improve Alberta for 15 years, and says he's confident the city will rebuild.

there. He has started a campaign to force landlords to clean up dilapidated homes and neglected property.

There's no question that the identities of the City Council member and the neighborhood are linked. He's

See **ALBERTA** | 12A

Shelters, clinics take in displaced pets

By Mark Hughes Cobb and Katherine Lee

TUSCALOOSA | Cats hide very well. So most of the storm-displaced pets coming to the Tuscaloosa Metro Animal Shelter, and various veterinary clinics and hospitals in the area, are puppies and adult dogs.

"I think once the debris has been removed, the surface taken off, we'll be finding more cats," said Judy Hill, director at the shelter.

"We have had quite a few underaged kittens, and we've let them go to some rescue people who will bottle-feed them, because otherwise they wouldn't make it."

Although the shelter needs volunteers to help with intake, and dispensing food, litter and cleaning supplies, the early post-tornado response has been gratifying, she said.

Around 30 volunteers were helping on Saturday afternoon and others brought in dog food, toys and other supplies.

The U.S. Humane Society has set up the 205-397-8534 number as a database for lost-and-found animals. It'll be open 8 a.m.-5 p.m. daily. The national group is also sending two teams in, probably arriving Sunday, to assist the Tuscaloosa Department of Transportation Animal Control

STAFF PHOTO | MICHELLE LEPIANKA CARTER
Kelley Strickland, shelter manager at Tuscaloosa Metro Animal Shelter, visits a displaced pregnant dog at the shelter on Saturday. The shelter has no power and needs volunteers.

See **PETS** | 11A

MISSING A PET OR FOUND A LOST ONE?

■ To help locate your pet, or help an animal get back to its owner, call the Humane Society's database at 205-397-8534, 8 a.m. to 5 p.m. daily. Information collected there will be emailed to area shelters.

■ If you have lost or found an animal, you can also visit www.altornadoanimals.wordpress.com, or send email to tornadopetsofal@yahoo.com. That group of animal-welfare agencies is gathering info and photos, and posting them on Facebook, Twitter and elsewhere to try and help owners find pets.

■ **Foster care:** T-Town Paws is trying to find people to foster pets who've been displaced. Contact them at 205-752-1931, or visit at www.t-townpaws.org.

■ **Help needed:** Tuscaloosa Metro Animal Shelter, at 3140 35th St., needs volunteers. Power is out right now, so don't call. They'll be open roughly 10 a.m.-7 p.m. today. Because of work in the heavily damaged areas on 35th Street, those attempting to reach the animal shelter should take Joe Malisham Parkway to Martin Luther King Jr. Boulevard, which crosses 35th Street. www.metroanimalshelter.org.

High 88 Low 60

43

ABOVE: Actor Charlie Sheen shakes hands with Jerry Funderburk. Sheen came to town to tour Tuscaloosa's storm devastated areas. He started in Alberta and made visits to 15th Street, the University of Alabama and the Belk Center.

Robert Sutton/The Tuscaloosa News

RIGHT: Mayor Walt Maddox and Charlie Sheen answer questions from the media on May 2.

Robert Sutton/The Tuscaloosa News

ABOVE: Volunteers at Tuscaloosa Magnet School on May 2 prepare to move materials salvaged from Alberta Elementary, which was destroyed. *Michelle Lepianka Carter/The Tuscaloosa News*

LEFT: Volunteer Parker Barrineau creates bead jewelry with Kaleb Ryan, 6, at the shelter set up inside the VA Medical Center on May 2. Kaleb was staying at the shelter with his family after the tornado destroyed their home. *Michelle Lepianka Carter/The Tuscaloosa News*

OPPOSITE: Shea McElroy, left, and Candace Williams, right, stack canned goods on May 2, in Brookwood. The volunteers at the G.G. Hardin Center were organizing donated items to be used in the storm recovery effort. *Robert Sutton/The Tuscaloosa News*

ABOVE: Immediately after the storm, about 240 local residents stayed in the shelter set up at the Belk Center, according to Kristiana Kocis, public information officer for the Red Cross. *Michelle Lepianka Carter/The Tuscaloosa News*

OPPOSITE: Children play at C.J.'s Bus outside the shelter set up at the Belk Center on May 2. C.J.'s Bus, from Evansville, Ind., provides 'playcare' for children displaced by a disaster, said executive director Kathryn Martin. *Michelle Lepianka Carter/The Tuscaloosa News*

ABOVE: The VA Medical Center set up a shelter inside their facility for those displaced by the tornado. *Michelle Lepianka Carter/The Tuscaloosa News*

OPPOSITE: Prince Rowe, a resident of the Holt community, sits on the edge of his bed inside the VA Medical Center on May 2. Rowe said his home was destroyed by the tornado. He moved to Tuscaloosa about a month and a half ago with the dream of opening a barbecue business. "I feel more like a survivor instead of a victim. You can always get more stuff," Rowe said about his experience.

Michelle Lepianka Carter/The Tuscaloosa News

OPPOSITE: Volunteers clean debris and rubble from a trailer park near Crescent Ridge Road in the Holt area on May 4. *Dusty Compton / The Tuscaloosa News*

BELOW: Northport Power Equipment mechanic Leo Pate, right, services a chainsaw as Husqvarna representative Mike Thrower, left, brings a new saw out at the shop in Northport, May 4. Northport Power Equipment sharpened chainsaws for free and helped customers with their tree-handling needs. "We just want to express our sympathy and support for those affected by the tornado. We're helping as much as possible," Northport Power Equipment owner Evelyn Ellis said. *Dusty Compton / The Tuscaloosa News*

53

RIGHT: A cross stands among debris and rubble that used to be buildings and homes in Alberta on May 5. *Michelle Lepianka Carter/The Tuscaloosa News*

BELOW & OPPOSITE: Kerry Kennedy of Fire Horse Studios throws Twister Tumblers at her Kentuck studio in Northport on May 6. Kennedy, who suffered damage to her cars and home in the tornado, said she wanted to give something back to the community, so she produced these tumblers and sold them for $15, with the proceeds being donated to tornado relief. *Robert Sutton/The Tuscaloosa News*

ABOVE: Volunteers distribute supplies to storm victims. *Dusty Compton/The Tuscaloosa News*

RIGHT: Shaun Donovan, secretary of Housing and Urban Development, and Mayor Walt Maddox tour Rosedale Court. The HUD secretary was joined by Maddox, Sen. Richard Shelby, U.S. Rep. Spencer Bachus and U.S. Rep. Terri Sewell. *Robert Sutton/The Tuscaloosa News*

TOP LEFT: Mayor Walt Maddox speaks to the media as Sen. Richard Shelby, left, and Shaun Donovan, right, stand by. *Robert Sutton/The Tuscaloosa News*

LEFT: Former 'N Sync star Lance Bass delivers supplies at the Leland Shopping Center in Tuscaloosa on May 9. *Dusty Compton/The Tuscaloosa News*

OPPOSITE: Country music star Hank Williams Jr. looks over the devastation at Soma Church in the Holt community on May 10. *Dusty Compton/The Tuscaloosa News*

BELOW: Sadie Robinson, 67, at her granddaughter's home in Tuscaloosa on May 10. She said she thanks God that she is alive after the April 27 tornado demolished her apartment. But she also has a few rescuers to thank, among them a 13-year-old boy. *Dusty Compton/The Tuscaloosa News*

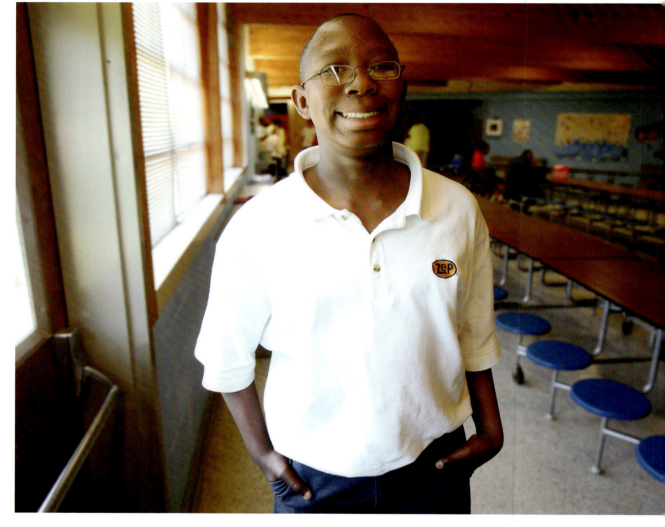

ABOVE: Jamarcus Golden, 13, is seen in Tuscaloosa, Wednesday, May 11. Jamarcus pulled Sadie Robinson, 67, from the rubble. *Dusty Compton/The Tuscaloosa News*

OPPOSITE: Jamarcus is hugged by his grandmother, Johnnie Graham, right, and aunt, Carrie Graham after telling his story of heroism. *Dusty Compton/The Tuscaloosa News*

ABOVE: Steve Ballard, left, Duke LoCicero, and Scott Ballard, right, prepare food at Midtown Village on May 11. Midtown Village, partnered with "Three Chefs, One Mission," to host a New Orleans-style tasting event on the green space. The event was an outreach effort to the first responders and all who were impacted by the tornado.

Dusty Compton/The Tuscaloosa News

LEFT: Former University of Alabama and current Atlanta Falcons NFL wide receiver Julio Jones, Lugene Gibbs, left, and Dan Lawler, right, unload supplies for the Red Cross at the Leland Shopping Center staging area in Alberta on May 12. *Dusty Compton/The Tuscaloosa News*

BELOW: Jeff Eichenlaub, of World Vision, left, Mike Carren and David Balos of JPMorgan Chase talk with Alabama native and NY Giants football player Justin Tuck, who is affiliated with World Vision, in the Hardee's parking lot on 15th Street on May 12. JPMorgan Chase pledged $100,000 to the Tuscaloosa Disaster Relief Fund and $5,000 to The Chamber of Commerce of West Alabama.

Michelle Lepianka Carter/The Tuscaloosa News

ABOVE: Uncle Kracker and Kenny Chesney performed at the Tuscaloosa Amphitheater on May 25. Proceeds went to relief efforts.

Dusty Compton/The Tuscaloosa News

OPPOSITE: Oma Phurrough, 97, holds a photograph of herself being taking away from her home, which was destroyed during the tornado, at her children's home in Northport on May 12. *Dusty Compton/The Tuscaloosa News*

RIGHT: Comedian Jeff Dunham performs with Walter at the Tuscaloosa Amphitheater on July 8. Dunham announced he would donate $50,000 to relief efforts. *Marion R Walding/The Tuscaloosa News*

OPPOSITE: Alabama native Ruben Studdard, left, takes a photograph with Annie Jones at the Salvation Army distribution center at McFarland Mall in Tuscaloosa on July 7. GMC, America's Favorite Channel for Uplifting Music and Entertainment, in partnership with Comcast Tuscaloosa and Feed the Children sponsored a Tuscaloosa tornado victims outreach event in conjunction with University City Church of Christ. This outreach is part of the GMC Uplift Someone America tour. Ruben Studdard, Grammy-nominated R&B, pop and gospel singer who rose to fame when he won the second season of "American Idol," joined outreach sponsors for the one-day event, which assisted 200 local families who were affected by the April 27 tornado. *Dusty Compton/The Tuscaloosa News*

ALBERTA FAMILY

STEPHANIE TAYLOR, STAFF WRITER

Amie Hall didn't know where she was when she crawled from the rubble of her home in the east Tuscaloosa community of Alberta on April 27.

Her home had been on 25th Avenue East, three houses down from the KFC at the corner of University Boulevard. It landed next to the ruins of Alberta Elementary School — at least a block and a half away.

"It was like we were floating," said Hall, 23.

Instinct set in. Hall said she managed to weave and balance her way through the house as it flew airborne down the block. She was clutching her cellphone, still connected to her husband, Keith Matthews, and holding her 10-month-old daughter, Krystin, close.

"It was like the wind was demanding to get her from me. She was talking and laughing. Things were flying and hitting both of us. There was no way I was going to let her go."

Khloe, 3, and Karter, 1, were taking naps in their bedroom. Khloe was thrown from the house when it landed, but suffered no injuries. Amazingly, Karter was still asleep when his mother made his way to his room.

"He was still on the mattress," Hall said. "The sheets had fallen off. I was thinking that he was dead and just ran up and started shaking him."

Amie didn't realize how severe the weather was until Keith called her that afternoon. He was driving on Hargrove Road near the Department of Public Health and saw the tornado as it crossed the central part of the city. She opened the front door, and saw a funnel cloud whipping toward the house.

Keith remained on the phone, terrified as he heard the house tumble down the street and his wife struggle to protect their children.

The phone went dead, and he began a harrowing two-hour journey home, dodging downed trees and police barricades. He eventually got to the Jim Myers Drug store on University Boulevard East, where he parked and began running.

"I could see a clear path to where my house once stood," he said. "But I couldn't recognize where it had been. I didn't see anyone that I knew, so I just started to look through the debris. Finally, I looked up and my dad, who had been up the street with my grandmother, came walking down the street."

The two started walking the neighborhood and found the house. Amie had set her cellphone down near the opening she had crawled from.

"I saw that, and it was so carefully placed, and I knew she had left it there," he said. "I knew she was all right."

The next several hours were chaotic, the couple said. Friends were watching the girls as Amie searched for an ambulance to treat Karter's injuries. They

---

OPPOSITE: Keith Matthews talks about the tornado with his wife, Amie Hall, and their children, Khloe Matthews, 3, Krystin, 10 months, and Karter, 1, inside the tornado relief shelter at the Belk Center Tuesday, May 3. The family's house in Alberta was lifted from its foundation during the tornado and dropped further away.

Michelle Lepianka Carter/The Tuscaloosa News

became separated and were passed along to other friends, adding to the confusion and panic. They didn't reunite until 1:30 a.m. It took three days for Amie to realize that her left foot had been broken by part of the house that crashed down on her when they landed.

The couple went to Alberta afterward and salvaged only one item from the wreckage — Amie's birth certificate.

"It still seems like a dream. There's no way you can explain the feeling at all," she said of the tornado and how it felt to go back to the neighborhood. "It's like we're in another world — like it's a bad dream or a movie. It's unreal." ■

TOP LEFT: Karter Matthews, 1, slept through the tornado even as it lifted his home into the air and dropped it away from its foundation.

Michelle Lepianka Carter/The Tuscaloosa News

TOP RIGHT: Krystin Matthews, 10 months, sleeps in her mother's arms at the tornado relief shelter at the Belk Center on May 3.

Michelle Lepianka Carter/The Tuscaloosa News

BOTTOM RIGHT: Khloe Matthews, 3, takes a long drink from her sippy cup.

Michelle Lepianka Carter/The Tuscaloosa News

ABOVE: Amie Hall, 23, holding daughter, Krystin, 10 months, talks about her experience during the tornado when her family's home was lifted into the air and dropped more than a block away while she and her children were inside. *Michelle Lepianka Carter/The Tuscaloosa News*

ABOVE: The Matthews family sit on their beds at the tornado relief shelter inside the Belk Center on May 3. *Michelle Lepianka Carter/The Tuscaloosa News*

OPPOSITE: Amie Hall tucks Krystin in for a nap at the shelter. *Michelle Lepianka Carter/The Tuscaloosa News*

ROBERT REED

ADAM JONES, STAFF WRITER

They weren't sure about him at first. His trailer was old and grungy, and Crescent Mobile Home Estates in Holt seemed to be fine without any more people.

Then Jeff Stewart, whose family owns the mobile home park off Keene Drive in Holt, made Robert Reed the park manager. One tenant told Stewart he wasn't going to pay his rent to an ex-convict. Instead, he'd mail his check.

But Reed won over Crescent Mobile Home Estates. He fixed up his trailer, his lot and built a new porch.

"It was the best-looking one out there," Stewart said.

Reed was a good park manager, too. He helped out with yard work and answered tenants' calls.

Now, Stewart and the other residents don't use words like "hero" and "superman" to describe Reed because he ended up being a swell super.

Rather, they call him a hero because he rescued many of them after the monster EF-4 tornado leveled the trailer park April 27. A lot of heroes were made that night throughout Tuscaloosa, but for the trailer park on the edge of town, Reed is theirs.

'ONE IN A MILLION'

Reed pulled 12 people from rubble that even he admits he doesn't know how he moved. Those who stayed in their mobile homes said Reed ran around the park looking for yet another person who needed saving, lifting appliances and brick walls with ease.

"He's a true hero, that's for sure," said John Hayes, who lives in the trailer park. "He just went with no regard to himself. He's one in a million."

The residents said it was fate, the belief that everything up to a certain point happens for a reason, and that reason was made clear in that moment. Reed said someone from the neighboring Soma of Christ Church told him God had prepared him for April 27. He was exactly where he needed to be.

Looking out over the nearly empty trailer park this week, Reed said he believes it, too.

"I really do," he said.

NOT A LIFE HE EXPECTED

Life in a trailer in Holt with his fiance and three children, scratching out a living with his hands and his lawn equipment, wasn't the life he'd envisioned as a starting quarterback for Aliceville High School in the early 1990s. One of his linemen, Walter Jones, went on to play college football at Florida State University and spent nine years in the NFL. Reed got a scholarship to play football at Iowa Wesleyan College, a small NAIA-associated liberal arts school.

But whether by circumstance or bad decisions,

OPPOSITE: Robert Reed is seen at the site of his home near Crescent Ridge Road in Tuscaloosa on May 19, 2011. Reed played football in college and kept up weightlifting in the years since. It paid off on April 27, as he used what witnesses call superhuman strength to pull people from the rubble of the trailer park where he was the property manager.

Dusty Compton/The Tuscaloosa News

ABOVE & OPPOSITE: Robert Reed, at Crescent Mobile Home Estates, which was destroyed by the tornado. *Dusty Compton/The Tuscaloosa News*

perhaps both, Reed never made many headlines in football and didn't graduate. He dropped out of Iowa Wesleyan to play football at a community college in Mississippi to be near a baby he was told was his, but wasn't. Reed later served more than seven years in a Mississippi prison for dealing and possessing drugs, a charge he said he took upon himself to save his girlfriend from losing custody of their children.

AFTER PRISON

Whatever the criminal details, Reed left prison a different man, set on being a good father and working hard to support them.

He came to Tuscaloosa and dated April Watson, his fiance, for a couple of years. He was fortunate Stewart went with his gut feeling about Reed's character, letting him move into Crescent Mobile Home Estates last year with a trailer older than the park's standards, and was fortunate again when Stewart looked past Reed's troubled background to make him park manager a few months later. Reed had already worked with Stewart, a firefighter, on several landscaping jobs and had proven handy in the trailer park.

"I told him, 'Robert, your past is your past, and that don't change how I feel about you,'" Stewart said. "He almost took that place over like he owned it, and I wanted him to."

The folks in Crescent Mobile Home Estates also believe Reed was cut out for rescue. After football, Reed never stopped working out. Even after prison, he worked out religiously five days a week. On an empty slab in the park, he could be found pumping iron on his bench, rain, shine or cold. He said he could bench 415 pounds before the tornado. It's clear from looking at him there is a chiseled mountain of strength under his shirt.

"Him being that strong really helped him that night," said Ronnie Morris, who's lived in the trailer park for 26 years. "He was absolutely freaking amazing."

Reed wasn't supposed to be at the trailer park during the tornado. Watson said their safety plan was to go to a relative's house, but they didn't make it out of the park.

"We got in the tub, and we started praying," Watson said. "I prayed that God would move the tornado over us. He didn't, but I said, 'Lord, keep my family safe,' and He did."

Watson said she doesn't remember anything that happened, but their daughter said she remembers Reed flying through the air trying to grab his niece,

who lives with them. His niece landed across the street in a field. Reed and his daughter landed in the street.

In the midst of the storm, a truck flew toward them, and Reed said he managed to cover his daughter as it flew over them, scraping his neck and hitting her in the face, causing a concussion.

After it passed, Reed said he saw Watson lying on the ground with their air-conditioning unit on top of her head. He ran to her and threw the unit off.

"Looked like she was gone, so I just got down on my knees and prayed," Reed said. "I went numb. I didn't notice nothing about my surroundings."

His daughter was screaming, "Momma," again and again, and then Watson opened her eyes and moved.

"When she opened her eyes, I just came alive," Reed said. "If she hadn't gotten up, I wouldn't have moved."

Watson would later need surgery for a foot that was almost sliced off and to remove sticks lodged in her head.

Reed moved Watson and their family into a ditch, believing another tornado was right behind. Then he heard Hayes calling for help.

Hayes, his wife and his mother were in their trailer experiencing their own hell. Another trailer had blown into theirs, and both had collapsed on top of them. Hayes managed to crawl out, but couldn't get to his family. A wall lay on top of them along with a refrigerator and a water heater.

"They couldn't push it up because all this heavy stuff on them," Reed said. "With the adrenaline

RIGHT: Robert Reed is seen at the site of his home near Crescent Ridge Road in Tuscaloosa on May 19.

Dusty Compton/The Tuscaloosa News

rushing it was really light, so I just picked it up and threw it."

Hayes said it was a big, double-door refrigerator, and moving it in any way except off the top of the pile could have further injured his wife and mother.

"He picks it up on its side like it was nothing, and threw it over," Hayes said. "I don't know how he done it, but you do extraordinary things that you don't know how in times like these."

By now, it was clear another twister wasn't coming, so Reed moved his wife and children into Soma Church, getting inside through a busted window. He put his 14-year-old son in charge of calling for help and told his daughter not to describe Watson's wound to her. Stay positive, he said.

"She asked if I was leaving her, and I said I gotta go help," Reed said. "She understood and told me to go."

He ran back into the trailer park, pulling people from the rubble and carrying them to the street or back to the church, the only structure left standing in what was now an open field.

'LAST BREATH'

Then he heard a call from a nearby house, the home of an 88-year-old woman, Annie Lois Sayer. Neighbors said she was trapped, but couldn't find her. Reed asked her to moan if she could, and spied her dress, realizing she was being crushed by two brick walls.

He lifted one off, and raised the other so someone else could pull Sayer out. They put her on a door, and Reed told her she was OK. Everything was going to be alright, he said.

"By the time we got to the road, she took her last breath," Reed said. "I see her every time I go to sleep. Every time I go to the trailer park, I see her. I know it's not sane, but I do."

He went back to Sayer's house days later, and found he couldn't budge the wall.

After helping Sayer, he rescued another man who had been tossed, along with his trailer, into a field. Now, ambulances and first responders had managed to find their way to Keene Drive, and Reed ran back to his family. Watson needed medical attention, but others more badly wounded took priority.

"I was fixin' to pick her up even if I had to walk all the way to DCH," he said.

Fortunately, a Tuscaloosa County Sheriff's deputy who was an acquaintance said he would take the family to DCH Regional Medical Center and make sure they got attention as if they were his own family, Reed said. He loaded them in the back of the police car, and went back to work, helping carry people to ambulances. He later got a ride to DCH to get the nasty scrape on his neck treated.

In the weeks since that night, an outpouring of thanks have descended on Reed, and he, along with his neighbors, who lost everything have been given so much.

Stewart kept him to help clear debris, but isn't sure his family will be able to afford to rebuild the trailer park. Insurance and FEMA need to weigh in, and Soma Church has offered to buy the property.

A month after the storm, Reed, was waiting, for FEMA to help with the medical bills. The lawn equipment that he made a living from was gone.

"I lost everything," he said. "It's putting me in a bind because that's how I support my family, but as long as my family is still alive, we can start back new."

Stewart has helped out some, and said Reed has not sought handouts or publicity.

"He's still just regular ol' Robert," Stewart said. ■

RECOVERY

AUGUST 8, 2011 | ADAM JONES, STAFF WRITER

A CUT TO THE BODY begins to heal immediately.

It doesn't seem like it at first. There's pain and tenderness that linger for days. But underneath, the body is working fervently to heal. Although the process is ugly and pain lingers, eventually the body repairs a wound, eliminating the threat.

Even months after the storm, families, businesses and entire neighborhoods are dealing with the aftermath, their lives forever changed, waiting for whatever the new normal will mean.

"We will be in recovery for the foreseeable future," said Tuscaloosa Mayor Walt Maddox. "I sense the mood of the city is one of optimism, but I think there is an understanding that there is a long way to go."

More than 90 percent of the 10 million cubic yards of debris has been removed across Alabama. The Federal Emergency Management Agency used the Alabama disaster to try out a new program in which the federal government paid for 90 percent of debris removal, instead of the usual 75 percent, in the first two months after the disaster. Dubbed Operation Clean Sweep, the program also fast-tracked debris removal from private property.

"We've actually set the standard and raised the bar for debris removal in a large-scale disaster," said Michael Byrne, FEMA's coordinating officer for the disaster in the state.

The Tuscaloosa City Council has allowed contractors to demolish damaged private properties. Initially this is voluntary, but eventually the city plans to switch to forced condemnation of uninhabitable property. County government will do likewise.

Despite the contests ahead, County Executive Hardy McCollum said he is pleased with the speed of recovery. "I feel very proud about where we are," he said.

The city hired a consultant and organized citizens into a committee to evaluate recommendations for a broad redevelopment plan, dubbed the "Tuscaloosa Forward" plan. A series of town hall meetings drew more than 1,000 residents. Others offered ideas on an interactive website.

The mayor recommended a plan that includes a winding trail that recalls the path of the storm through Tuscaloosa. It would be accessible to pedestrians and cyclists who could stop along way to reflect at markers that would memorialize the victims.

"We've got a lot of great ideas and we've got a big vision, and a lot of that was generated by the public. Now we're just trying to build off that," Maddox told The Tuscaloosa News in August.

At that point, the plan was headed toward final approval by the City Council. Even so, bringing that vision into reality was expected to involve many hurdles.

OPPOSITE: Graham Walters, 12, left, and his father, John Walters, help remove debris in the Holt community near Soma Church in Tuscaloosa, Saturday, May 21, 2011. Former Alabama coach Gene Stallings brought as many as 150 former players along with other volunteers to help clean up debris in the area. *Dusty Compton/The Tuscaloosa News*

The next step is rebuilding, and although some homes and businesses have been repaired or rebuilt, the areas the tornado swept through remain mostly barren.

Maddox said rebuilding will likely accelerate near the end of the year and begin in earnest in early 2012. Rebuilding will take years, he said.

"The sounds of hammers will become common course over the next several years," Maddox said.

Through the summer, survivors wrangled for insurance payments, loans and government aid. Before the deadline in July, 88,076 Alabamians and their families had applied for aid with FEMA, which can grant up to $30,200 to disaster victims to cover needs not met by insurance. Only 18 percent were initially approved.

Tuscaloosa County's approval rate is higher at 27 percent, and the county has received the most in FEMA grants. As of August, about $15 million had been awarded to 3,521 of the 12,936 applicants in the county.

"We are not declaring victory by any means," said Jeff Byard, FEMA's state coordinating officer. "We've got a lot of work to do."

What took a tornado six minutes to blow away will take months and years to restore.

"If we are truly to honor the memories of those whom we have lost, we are called upon to look at April 27 as a beginning and not an ending," Tuscaloosa Mayor Walt Maddox told the crowd at a memorial candle light vigil barely a month after the storm.

"How we fight back, how we refuse to quit and how we rebuild will ensure that we never forget our victims, our survivors, our heroes.

"In every new home that is constructed and business that is reopened, we will remember. In every church that is rebuilt and street that is transformed, we will remember."

"From Rosedale to Forest Lake, from Alberta to Holt, we have learned to set aside our differences and stand shoulder-to-shoulder with our fellow citizens regardless of race, religion, socioeconomic status or politics," Maddox said.

From a deep wound, a scar remains. The scar doesn't mean the wound didn't heal. The scar tissue is new tissue, the remnants of healing and restoration. That is what the people of Tuscaloosa and Alabama will long remember. ∎

ABOVE: Sandra Farris, left, and Donna Deal clean up the family's property on Crescent Ridge Road Friday, April 29. Deal said she and eight other people, along with about 11 dogs, were safely inside a storm shelter when the tornado destroyed their homes and business. *Michelle Lepianka Carter/The Tuscaloosa News*

ABOVE: Businesses left in rubble along McFarland Boulevard after a tornado ripped through Tuscaloosa, Wednesday, April 27.
Michelle Lepianka Carter/The Tuscaloosa News

LEFT: President Barack Obama's helicopter circles over the devastated Forest Lake neighborhood Friday, April 29.
Michelle Lepianka Carter/The Tuscaloosa News

BELOW: Forest Lake on Friday, April 29. *Stephanie Taylor/The Tuscaloosa News*

ABOVE: Martha Deal hugs her grandson Matt Deal as they clean up the family's property along Crescent Ridge Road Friday, April 29. The family's two homes and business, Marine Repair, were destroyed by Wednesday's tornado. Matt and his finance, Caleigh Tyner, were supposed to be getting married today. Their wedding and honeymoon have been postponed. Her dress and some other wedding items were inside one of the destroyed homes. *Michelle Lepianka Carter/The Tuscaloosa News*

OPPOSITE: Huston Walters, 20, a sophomore at the University of Alabama from Navarre, Fla., takes a break from cleaning up at his home in the Forest Lake neighborhood Friday, April 29. Walters was at home talking to his mother, Marisa, on his cell phone taking shelter in the bathroom. It was the only room in the house intact. *Michelle Lepianka Carter/The Tuscaloosa News*

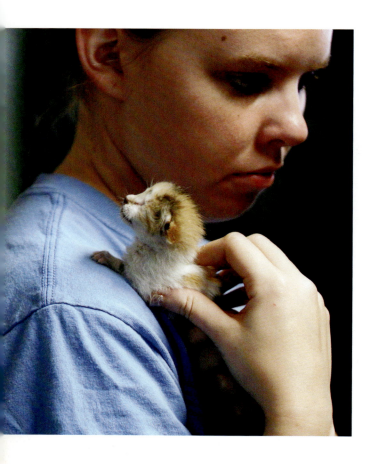

ABOVE: Miranda Workman, an employee at Metro Animal Shelter, holds a 2-week-old kitten rescued after the tornado. *Michelle Lepianka Carter/The Tuscaloosa News*

RIGHT: Mike Hall hangs a flag on a post at Eagle Cove Marina. Several boats and the marina suffered extensive damage as a result of the storm.

Robert Sutton/The Tuscaloosa News

ABOVE: Matt Deal, left, Donna Deal and Kevin Lake pick up pieces of a house as they clean up the family's property along Crescent Ridge Road Friday, April 29. The family's two homes and business, Marine Repair, were destroyed by the tornado. *Michelle Lepianka Carter/The Tuscaloosa News*

ABOVE: Brandon Cook attaches an Alabama flag and American flag to what's left of a tree near Lisa Stacy's mother's home in the Holt community Friday, April 29. *Michelle Lepianka Carter/The Tuscaloosa News*

RIGHT: Members of the Alberta Baptist Church congregation pray during church service that was held in the parking lot next to the church on Sunday morning, four days after the storm. The church suffered major structural damage. *T.G. Paschal/The Tuscaloosa News*

ABOVE: The RaceWay on Veterans Memorial Parkway reopened in Tuscaloosa, Thursday, May 5.

Dusty Compton/The Tuscaloosa News

TOP RIGHT: Krispy Kreme has a sign claiming their return in Tuscaloosa, Thursday, May 5.

Dusty Compton/The Tuscaloosa News

RIGHT: The Belk department store in the University Mall reopened in Tuscaloosa, Thursday, May 5.

Dusty Compton/The Tuscaloosa News

ABOVE: TSC Service and Supply advertises their availability in the wake of the tornado. *Robert Sutton/The Tuscaloosa News*

OPPOSITE: The new federal courthouse will include 16 murals painted by artist Caleb O'Conner depicting historic moments in Tuscaloosa history including one mural depicting the recent tornado.

Robert Sutton/The Tuscaloosa News

ABOVE: Paul Hinson with Hanks Auto Glass Inc. repairs the drivers-side window on a Mercury Grand Marquis on Thursday morning May 19. Hank's Auto Glass, along with similar businesses in the Tuscaloosa community, has been working extra hours trying to take care of customers affected by the recent tornado.

Robert Sutton/The Tuscaloosa News

RIGHT: Hank McLaughlin prepares a piece of auto glass for installation at his shop on Thursday May 19.

Robert Sutton/The Tuscaloosa News

OPPOSITE: Josh Calhoun, left, Jeff Frazier, center, and Robert Knight, right, remove a damaged window frame from a business in Midtown. Workers with TPG Glass prepare the front of Tazikis in Midtown for new windows on Thursday morning May 19.

Robert Sutton/The Tuscaloosa News

TOP LEFT: University of Alabama head football coach Nick Saban, right, speaks with Teddy Rowe, left, and daughter Helen Sims at the site of a home in the Holt community Friday, May 20. Nick and Terry Saban donated $50,000 to help rebuild the home of Teddy and Rosie Rowe. *Dusty Compton/The Tuscaloosa News*

LEFT: Ginger Brookover gives a teddy bear to Releigh McCall, 22 months, at Tender Loving Care daycare in Tuscaloosa, Friday, May 20. Brookover, who is from Morgantown, W. Va., collected more than 100 new teddy bears to bring to children in Tuscaloosa. "I saw the tornado on television and the first thing I though about was the children, so here I am," Brookover said. *Dusty Compton/The Tuscaloosa News*

OPPOSITE: Jeff Frazier removes a damaged window frame from a business in Midtown. TPG is just one of several similar businesses who have been busy repairing homes businesses and vehicles since the April 27 tornado. *Robert Sutton/The Tuscaloosa News*

ABOVE: Volunteers help remove debris in the Holt community near Soma Church in Tuscaloosa, Saturday, May 21. Former Alabama coach Gene Stallings brought as many as 150 former players along with other volunteers to help clean up debris in the area. *Dusty Compton/The Tuscaloosa News*

OPPOSITE: Gene Stallings, left, and Shannon Brown, right, overlook the debris in the Holt community near Soma Church in Tuscaloosa, Saturday, May 21. *Dusty Compton/The Tuscaloosa News*

ABOVE: Travis Wilson, left, Natalie Gibson and Laura Kathryn Murphy, right, watch the Alabama vs. Memphis college softball game near a large tornado support ribbon in Tuscaloosa, Saturday, May 21. *Dusty Compton/The Tuscaloosa News*

LEFT: Susan Pate meets Tommy Mobley for the first time seated beside her husband, Corporal Mickey Pate of the Tuscaloosa Sheriff's Department, after an award ceremony recognizing individuals in the sheriff's department and community for acts of heroism during the April 27 tornado at the Sheriff's Office hangar at the Tuscaloosa Regional Airport Tuesday, May 24. Corporal Pate rescued Mobley in the 15th Street area. *Michelle Lepianka Carter/The Tuscaloosa News*

BELOW: A litter of puppies waits inside an air-conditioned tent to be claimed by their owner after being rescued and brought to the Tuscaloosa Metro Animal Shelter Tuesday, May 24. The shelter was full of animals displaced by the tornado. Two tents were set up behind the shelter with outdoor air-conditioners to provide extra shelter for at least 50 more dogs when needed. *Michelle Lepianka Carter/The Tuscaloosa News*

ABOVE & LEFT: More than 1,000 people attended the Spirit of Tuscaloosa Candlelight Vigil held at Government Plaza on June 1. The event featured music from the Tuscaloosa Symphony Orchestra, bagpipes and several speakers including local law enforcement and Mayor Walt Maddox. The event ended with the lighting of candles and a slide show.
Robert Sutton/The Tuscaloosa News

OPPOSITE: Alabama Gov. Robert Bentley talks with Madison Shaw, 6, at the site of Mike and Ed's Barbecue on 15th Street in Tuscaloosa, Friday, May 27. Gov. Bentley spoke in Tuscaloosa Friday to mark the one month anniversary of the deadly tornado.
Dusty Compton/The Tuscaloosa News

ABOVE & RIGHT: Mayor Walt Maddox was greeted with a standing ovation by those in attendance at Wednesday night's candlelight vigil.

Robert Sutton/The Tuscaloosa News

OPPOSITE: The Richard A. Curry Building was severely damaged by the April 27 tornado that ripped through Tuscaloosa. *Michelle Lepianka Carter/The Tuscaloosa News*

ABOVE: NBA player Dwight Howard of the Orlando Magic meets fans at Snow Hinton Park Friday, June 3. Howard was at the community gathering in conjunction with members of Boys State helping with tornado relief as well as refurbishing a playground at Snow Hinton. *Michelle Lepianka Carter/The Tuscaloosa News*

LEFT: New York-based apparel manufacturer Alfred Dunner is donating tens of thousands of new women's garments in a wide range of sizes to Alabama tornado survivors. The donation includes products from the Alfred Dunner and Sunset Rd. spring and summer lines. The clothes were unloaded at Central High School by members of Central's football team and other volunteers on June 6.
Robert Sutton/The Tuscaloosa News

FAR LEFT: Babs Davis with the University of Alabama's college of Human Environmental Sciences catalogues clothing at the gym at Central High School.
Robert Sutton/The Tuscaloosa News

ABOVE: Danny Huffman meets Sgt. Derrick Riddle, right, and Lt. Tim Gray of Tuscaloosa Fire and Rescue Service, for the first time since the men pulled Huffman out of the rubble of the Labor Ready building. *Michelle Lepianka Carter/The Tuscaloosa News*

LEFT: Central High School sophomore Marshawn Leatherwood carries boxes of clothing donated by New York-based apparel manufacturer Alfred Dunner. *Robert Sutton/The Tuscaloosa News*

OPPOSITE: Danny Huffman, right, seated beside Sgt. Derrick Riddle of Tuscaloosa Fire and Rescue Service, talks about his experience during the tornado at Wings U Tuesday, June 7. Robert Harless, branch manager of Labor Ready, arrived at the scene and found Huffman trapped in the rubble and called Lt. Tim Gray and Sgt. Riddle to help as they were passing the scene. *Michelle Lepianka Carter/The Tuscaloosa News*

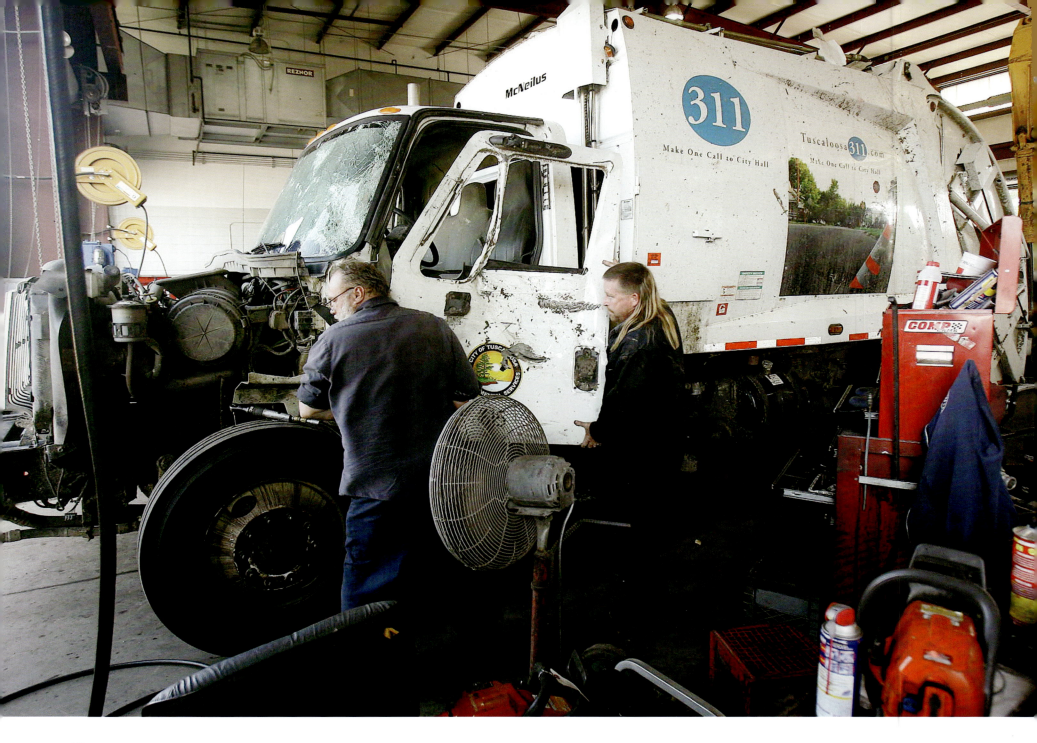

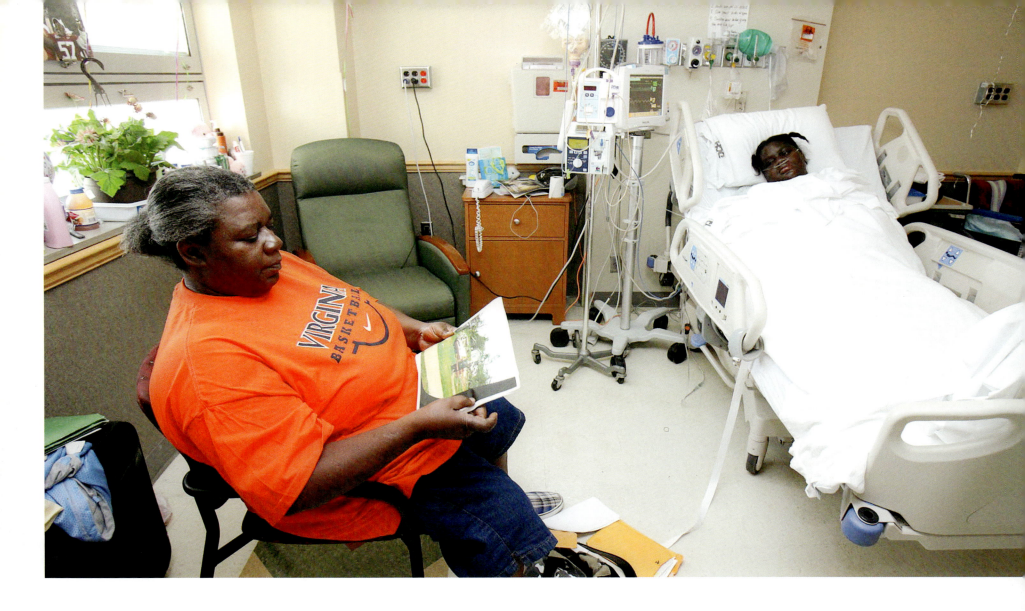

ABOVE: Shirley Howard, left, looks at a picture of the house she and daughter Monique, 24, right, were in when the April 27th tornado passed through her neighborhood at DCH Regional Medical Center in Tuscaloosa, Tuesday, June 14. Monique was one of two tornado victims still at DCH. *Dusty Compton/The Tuscaloosa News*

OPPOSITE: Daryl Kent, left, a TDOT mechanic for 26 years, and Jarrod Rice, a TDOT mechanic for eight years, replace a door on one of the city's trucks on Tuesday, June 14. *Michelle Lepianka Carter/The Tuscaloosa News*

ABOVE: St. Joe's players take on Northridge during a 7-on-7 scrimmage game at Northridge High School in Tuscaloosa, Wednesday, June 8. St. Joe's Catholic High School in Philadelphia, Penn., came to Tuscaloosa to help with tornado recovery and then held a practice session with Northridge and Holt. *Dusty Compton/The Tuscaloosa News*

LEFT: A memorial set up in the field across the street from where the house Carson Tinker, long snapper for the University of Alabama, lived along 25th Street that was destroyed by the April 27 tornado is seen Thursday, June 23. Tinker's girlfriend, Ashley Harrison, and their two dogs were killed during the storm. *Michelle Lepianka Carter/The Tuscaloosa News*

ABOVE: St. Joe's players celebrate after a winning session during a the scrimmage game. *Dusty Compton/The Tuscaloosa News*

RIGHT: Members of the faith-based volunteer group World Changers tear down homes near 28th Avenue that were heavily damaged by the April 27 tornado. *Michelle Lepianka Carter/The Tuscaloosa News*

THOSE WHO DIED

Here is a list of those whose deaths resulted from the April 27 tornado. This is the city of Tuscaloosa's official list, last updated on Sept. 13.

- Minnie Acklin, 73
- Jeffrey Artis, 51
- Brandon Scott Atterton, 23, of Bryant, Ala.
- Jenifer V. Bayode, 36
- Michael Bowers, 3
- Loryn Alexandra Brown, 21, of Wetumpka, Ala.
- Darlene Mary Bryant, 43
- Hugh Graham Davie, 55
- Ta'Christianna Dixon, 8 months
- Danielle Downs, 24, of Decatur, Ala.
- Makayla Edwards, 5
- Arielle Edwards, 22
- Melgium Farley, 58
- Cedria Harris, 9
- Keyshawn Harris, 5
- Ashley T. Harrison, 21, of Dallas, Texas
- Annie Lois Sayer, 88
- Shena Hutchins, 26
- Carolyn Ann Jackson, 50
- Jacqueline "Jackie" Myles Jefferson, 45
- Thelma Krallman, 89
- Mozelle Lancaster, 95
- Davis Lynn Lathem, 57
- Velma T. Leroy, 64
- Thomas D. Lewis, 66
- Dorothy Lewis, 61
- Eyvonne Mayes
- Christian A'lexis McNeil, 1
- Zyqueria McShan, 2
- Melanie Nicole Mixon, 21, of Mulga, Ala.
- Perry Blake Peek, 24
- Lola Pitts, 85
- Terrilyn Plump, 38
- Kevin Rice, 36
- Judy Sherrill, 62
- Morgan Sigler, 23, of Bryant, Ala.
- Will Stevens, of Somerville, Ala.
- Justin Leeric Thomas, 15
- Patricia Turner, 55
- William Lee Turner III
- Marcus J. Smith, of Richmond, Va.
- Kaiden McKinley Tyrell Blair, 2 months
- William Robert McPherson Jr., 85
- Leota Elaine Jones, 97
- Robert Gene Hicks, 83
- Helen M. Kemp, 80
- Lee Andrew Lee, 88
- Helen Wurm, 98
- Colvin "Corky" Rice, 78
- Ovella P. Andrews
- Calvin Hannah, 81

OPPOSITE: Members of the Alberta Baptist Church congregation pray during a church service that was held in the parking lot next to the church. *T.G. Paschal/The Tuscaloosa News*

AMPHITHEATER BENEFITS

MAY 25, AUG. 19, SEPT. 2, 2011 | MARK HUGHES COBB, STAFF WRITER

Tuscaloosa christened its municipal amphitheater to a stormy season, but the musical stars aligned as a number of big acts signed on for benefit concerts – including the first full concert by the band Alabama in several years.

The Tuscaloosa Amphitheater held its opening weekend with The Avett Brothers and Band of Horses April 1, and The O'Jays and Patti LaBelle April 2, the next show scheduled was hotly anticipated by country fans, with hit-making group Sugarland bringing its large-scale "Incredible Machine" tour to town April 15.

But tornados struck that day, damaging several local neighborhoods. Skies mostly cleared by early evening, but even though the Amphitheater itself sustained only minor damage and Sugarland was ready to go on, Mayor Walt Maddox was forced to call the show off. Too much of the city's personnel and resources had to be poured into emergency services.

Two weeks later, when the big tornado event hit, there was no show scheduled. Still the amphitheater served as a meeting and feeding point for workers and volunteers, feeding thousands through its new kitchens, designed to function for shows with up to 7,470 in attendance.

Kenny Chesney started the charity ball rolling with his May 25 concert. He'd first considered cancelling, what with the ongoing relief efforts, but the mayor assured the country superstar that Tuscaloosa could use an evening's break. So they played, and Chesney, his band, management and booking representatives donated their fees to GiveTuscaloosa.com.

"The heart of the country is with everybody who's dealing with this tragedy," Chesney said in a recorded statement. "And I'm thrilled, and we're thrilled that all the money from this show will stay in the community of Tuscaloosa. And we're looking really forward to doing the show."

It was a much-needed party, and delivered a lump-in-the-throat catharsis when Chesney lead a singalong on the band Alabama's ballad "My Home's in Alabama."

Others caught the idea.

Sugarland, unable to reschedule their show here, cut a new live version of their song "Stand Up" as a fund-raiser for both Tuscaloosa and Joplin, Mo. tornado relief. Boxer Deontay Wilder turned his June 18 bout into a disaster-relief benefit. The Aug. 19 show with My Morning Jacket, Neko Case and Phosphorescence was performed as a benefit for United Way of West Alabama's ongoing relief efforts.

"I think that's just why we're on the planet, to help each other," said MMJ lead singer and songwriter Jim James. "Everybody has up periods and down periods.

OPPOSITE: Uncle Kracker and Kenny Chesney play to a full house at the Tuscaloosa Amphitheater on May 25. *Dusty Compton/The Tuscaloosa News*

You have periods where you're down and need help, and then then we have periods where we're feeling good and able to help. It's just like the circle of life again,"

Probably the biggest-dollar benefit news at the amphitheater after Chesney, was that Alabama, which officially retired in 2004, would reunite for its first full concert in seven years as a tornado-relief benefit Sept. 2. Alabama had earlier in the summer headlined an all-star benefit concert at the BJCC in Birmingham, but the group only played a handful of songs, backed by members of the Tuscaloosa Symphony Orchestra. The TSO also backed Alabama at its amphitheater date.

Looking at ticket proceeds — the concert was a hard sellout the first weekend the tickets went on sale, bigger even than Chesney's May 25 concert — Maddox estimated the money raised would be more than $100,000.

"And that's a conservative estimate," he said.

The city donated 25 percent of concession sales back to tornado efforts; the city of Tuscaloosa generally takes 55 percent of amphitheater concession sales.

"I think it's going to be a good night for tornado-relief efforts, and a good night for music," Maddox said. "A good night for everybody."

Other upcoming shows are also contributing. Widespread Panic donated a portion of its Sept. 30 proceeds, and $5 from every ticket sold for the Pretty Lights, STS9 and Big Gigantic show Oct. 13 was set aside for the the Tuscaloosa Disaster Relief Fund. The event featured performances by Pretty Lights and special guests STS9 and Big Gigantic. Pretty Lights agreed to donate $5 from every ticket sold to the Tuscaloosa Disaster Relief Fund. The Tuscaloosa Amphitheater has a capacity of more than 7,000. ■

ABOVE: Jim James, lead singer of My Morning Jacket, hit the Tuscaloosa Ampthitheater stage on Aug. 19, as a benefit for the United Way of West Alabama's tornado relief fund.
Alicia Lavender/The Tuscaloosa News

ABOVE RIGHT: Randy Owen of the band Alabama performs Sept.2. The concert was expected to raise more than $100,000 for storm relief.
Marion R Walding/The Tuscaloosa News

RIGHT: Neko Case, left, joined My Morning Jacket at the Amp on Aug. 19. *Alicia Lavender/The Tuscaloosa News*

OPPOSITE: Kenny Chesney told the crowd, "The whole world knows this town is hurting. And the fact you came to see us play means a whole lot of money is going to help Tuscaloosa." *Dusty Compton/The Tuscaloosa News*

ABOVE: Jeff Cook of the band Alabama performs during their show Sept. 2. *Marion R Walding/The Tuscaloosa News*

RIGHT: Uncle Kracker opens for Kenny Chesney at the Tuscaloosa Amphitheater on May 25. *Dusty Compton/The Tuscaloosa News*

OPPOSITE: The Sept. 2 concert was the only full show the band Alabama has held since it officially retired several years ago. The Tuscaloosa Symphony Orchestra also performed. *Marion R Walding/The Tuscaloosa News*

BEFORE AND AFTER

THREE AREAS HIT HARD BY THE TORNADO: BEFORE AND AFTER

May 5, 2011. *Michelle Lepianka Carter/The Tuscaloosa News*

June 21, 2011. *Michelle Lepianka Carter/The Tuscaloosa News*

ABOVE: This is 25th Avenue in Alberta, seen before the tornado in an image from Google maps. As a reference point, the "Only" lettering in the street, on the right side of the photo can be seen in the "after" photos. *Google.com*

Sept. 19, 2011. *Michelle Lepianka Carter/The Tuscaloosa News*

ABOVE: This is Hokkaido Japanese Restaurant, 528 15th St., as it was seen before the April 27 tornado, in this image taken from Google maps. *Google.com*

May 5, 2011. *Michelle Lepianka Carter/Tuscaloosa News*

June 21, 2011. *Michelle Lepianka Carter/Tuscaloosa News*

July 28, 2011. *Michelle Lepianka Carter/Tuscaloosa News*

Sept. 19, 2011. *Michelle Lepianka Carter/Tuscaloosa News*

ABOVE: This is Rosedale Court, on 10th Avenue, before the tornado destroyed it, as seen on Google maps. As a point of reference, the blue phone booth near the center of the photo can be seen in photos taken after the storm. *Google.com*

May 5, 2011. *Michelle Lepianka Carter/Tuscaloosa News*

June 21, 2011. *Michelle Lepianka Carter/Tuscaloosa News*

July 28, 2011. *Michelle Lepianka Carter/Tuscaloosa News*

Sept. 19, 2011. *Michelle Lepianka Carter/Tuscaloosa News*

ACKNOWLEDGMENTS

FIRST RESPONSE TEAM

Tuscaloosa News journalists who provided coverage in the immediate aftermath of the April 27 tornado

Michelle Lepianka Carter
Staff Photographer

Mark Hughes Cobb
Staff Writer

Dusty Compton
Staff Photographer

Robert DeWitt
Staff Writer

Wayne Grayson
Staff Writer

Adam Jones
Staff Writer

Jason Morton
Staff Writer

Cory Pennington
Online Content Producer

Patrick Rupinski
Staff Writer

Jamon Smith
Staff Writer

Stephanie Taylor Murray
Staff Writer

NEWSROOM STAFF OF THE TUSCALOOSA NEWS

Lydia Seabol Avant, Lauren Barrera, Dana Beyerle, Anthony Bratina, Andrew Carroll, Michelle Lepianka Carter, Mark Hughes Cobb, Dusty Compton, Corey Craft, Robert DeWitt, Tommy Deas, Shweta Gamble, Chase Goodbread, Keli Goodson, Wayne Grayson, Cecil Hurt, Michael James, Peggy Johnson, Adam Jones, Katherine Lee, Damien Martin, Jason Morton, Greg Ostendorf, Cory Pennington, Chris Rattey, Douglas Ray, Brian Reynolds, Ken Roberts, Amy Robinson, Patrick Rupinski, Alex Scarborough, Ernie Shipe, Sean Shore, Betty Slowe, Jamon Smith, Edwin Stanton, Tommy Stevenson, Harold Stout, Janet Sudnik, Aaron Suttles, Robert Sutton, Stephanie Taylor Murray, John Wallace